WHY THE KING JAMES BIBLE

Authorized Version 1611

IS THE PERFECT WORD OF GOD

A Five Lesson Bible Study

Gary Miller
Edited by David W. Daniels

Copies available in the U.S. at your local Christian bookstore. Outside the U.S., visit **www.chick.com** for the most current list of distributors near you. Or call us at (909) 987-0771.

Copyright © 2006 by Gary Miller

Published by:
CHICK PUBLICATIONS
P.O. Box 3500, Ontario, CA 91761-1019 USA
Tel: (909) 987-0771
Fax: (909) 941-8128
Web: www.chick.com
Email: postmaster@chick.com
Printed in the United States of America

ISBN: 0-758906-63-3

These five lessons will help Christians understand that the Authorized Version, known as the King James Bible, is truly God's preserved words for English-speaking people.

God's very words are under attack, and have been, ever since Satan corrupted them when he talked to Eve in the Garden of Eden.

The apostle Paul tells us in 2 Corinthians 2:17:

> "For we are not as many, which corrupt the word of God: but as of sincerity, but as of God, in the sight of God speak we in Christ."

We hope you will find this study to be enlightening and edifying.

Gary and Lynda Miller

For additional Bible study materials for children and adults, please visit:

www.grace-harbor-church.org

Psalm 12:6-7

"The words of the LORD are pure words: as silver tried in a furnace of earth, purified seven times. Thou shalt keep them, O LORD, thou shalt preserve them from this generation for ever."

We do have a faithful God. We can rely upon Him to keep His promises. These verses clearly teach that our God has promised to keep and preserve His words.

Salvation

God's most important word to you is about your need for salvation. God's word tells us plainly and simply that we are sinners in need of a Saviour. God paid for our sin on Calvary's cross when the Lord Jesus Christ, God's only begotten Son, died for our sin. Our apostle Paul reveals the saving message of the gospel in I Corinthians 15:3-4:

"For I delivered unto you first of all that which I also received, how that Christ died for our sins according to the scriptures; And that he was buried, and that he rose again the third day according to the scriptures:"

Jesus' precious blood paid for our sins:

> "In whom we have redemption through his blood, the forgiveness of sins, according to the riches of his grace;" Ephesians 1:7

This is the message of the gospel of grace that we need to believe to be saved. Ephesians 2:8-9 tells us that salvation is by grace through faith and not by our works.

Have you trusted in the Lord Jesus Christ as your Saviour? If so, praise the Lord. If not, place your trust in Him right now.

The Purpose of This Book

The Bible is God's book. He gave it by inspiration. The words of scripture are God's words. But not only did God *give* His words to man, He also promised to *preserve them…* for specific reasons. They are shown to us in the Bible. We believe that we have the perfectly preserved words of God in our 1611 King James Bible, also called the "Authorized Version" or KJV.

Today, hundreds of books *call* themselves Bibles. We will see, in the following lessons, why they cannot *all* be the words of God and why only the 1611 KJV is God's perfectly preserved words in English.

Here are four important statements. In this book, you will learn what they mean.

1. God **Inspired** His words – God communicated His words perfectly through holy men of God.

2. God **Preserved** His words – God kept His inspired text safe throughout all ages, without loss or error.

3. God has a **Purpose** for His words – God's words tell us how we are to use them.

4. God's **Inspired and Perfectly Preserved Words in English** are known as the 1611 King James Bible.

Note: You will need a King James Bible
to fill in the blanks for these lessons.

LESSON 1

God Inspired His Words

"***All scripture is given by inspiration of God***, and is profitable for doctrine, for reproof, for correction, for instruction in righteousness: That the man of God may be perfect, throughly furnished unto all good works"

2 Timothy 3:16-17 tells us that all scripture (not some or most) is inspired by God. That's right. **All** scripture is inspired. Every verse from Genesis 1:1 to Revelation 22:21 is given by inspiration of God.

What Does "Inspiration of God" Mean?

God spoke into the hearts of His people what to write down. So the words of the scriptures (the Bible) are not the words of those men. They are God's own words, written down by the people He chose.

What Does "Scripture" Mean?

"Scripture" means "writing." But what does "scripture" mean in the Bible? The Bible defines its own words, and Matthew 22:29-31 defines the word "scripture":

> "Jesus answered and said unto them, Ye do err,
>
> not knowing the _____,
>
> nor the power of God… have ye not read that
>
> which was _____ unto you by
>
> _____…" (verses 29, 31)

When we talk about the Bible, "scripture" refers to the words written down that were spoken or revealed by God.

Are Only the "Originals" Inspired? What About the Copies?

Many people say that only the *"original autographs"* (the original tablets, animal skins or manuscripts physically written by Moses, David, Paul, etc.) were "inspired," but that copies made from these originals contain errors and are not reliable. ***This is a lie!*** The scriptures do tell us that the original manuscripts were inspired. But God also had His people make <u>faithful **copies** of these original manuscripts to keep His perfect words available to man</u>.

Check for yourself! You can find the word "scripture" in 53 verses of the Bible. <u>Not one of them ever refers to the "original</u>." Each is referring to *copies*. God calls those *copies* "scripture."

LOOK AT LUKE 4:16-21

"And he began to say unto them, This day is

this _____ fulfilled in

your ears." (verse 21)

Christ read from the book of Esaias (Isaiah). And He called ***the copy that He read from*** "scripture," the words of God.

READ JOHN 5:39

"Search the _____; for in

them ye think ye have eternal life: and they

are they which _____ of me."

Would Jesus Christ tell them "Search the scriptures" if they didn't have them?

(Circle the correct answer.)

Yes / No

Remember, these "scriptures" were *copies* of the originals.

READ LUKE 24:13-45

"And beginning at Moses and all the prophets,

he expounded unto them in all the

_____ the things concerning

himself." (verse 27)

During His ministry the Lord Jesus Christ *never read the originals.* He only read copies. But He called those copies _____. And they were *exact copies* of

God's actual words. Jesus never pointed out a single mistake in them. And if *anyone* would know, it would be God's own Son! After all, He is the one who spoke those very words to His prophets in the first place!

For *copies* to be scripture, they need to be perfect.

2 Timothy 3:16-17 says that all scripture was given to us by God. The scripture is the work of God. And God's work is perfect (Deuteronomy 32:4).

How Did the Lord Jesus Use the Word "Scripture"?

1　Christ knew the scriptures did not contain errors, because He is God. And God knows everything (see Colossians 2:2-3).

2　If Christ knew the scriptures had errors, He would not cover them up, because He is God. And God is holy and trustworthy and righteous. God cannot lie (see Titus 1:2).

3　Christ used *copies* of the scripture. He knew those copies were perfect. Christ used *all*, not just some, of the scriptures (see Luke 24:27). This shows His confidence that God's words were preserved. Exact copies are the preserved words of God.

Does the Bible say that **only** the "original autographs" are God's words?

(Circle the correct answer.)

Yes　/　No

Does the Bible say that you **cannot** trust an exact copy of God's words?

(Circle the correct answer.)

Yes / No

The Bible is clear. Trustworthy *copies* of God's words are called "scripture" over and over again.

READ 2 TIMOTHY 3:15

"And that from a child thou hast known the

holy _____..."

God called Timothy's copies _____.

READ ACTS 8:35

"Then Philip opened his mouth, and began at

the same _____, and preached

unto him Jesus."

God called the copy of Isaiah that was used by the Ethiopian Eunuch _____.

READ ACTS 17:2

"And Paul, as his manner was, went in unto them,

and three Sabbath days reasoned with them out

of the _____ ...."

God called the copies that were used by Jews in the synagogues _____. **These were copies.** But God called them "scriptures."

In Acts 18:24-28, we see that _____ was mighty in the _____ (verse 24).

In Acts 18:28 the scriptures were to _____ the Jews that Jesus was Christ. Apollos knew the scriptures. And he used them for a great purpose: to convince people that _____ is _____, their promised Saviour.

Summary

All scripture was given by the inspiration of God. "Inspiration" means that God spoke His words into the writers' hearts. So what they wrote were not man's words, but the words of God. The written words of God are called "scripture."

God inspired the scripture. The writings handwritten by Moses, the prophets and apostles are all scripture and are inspired. But exact copies and correct translations are *also* called scripture. They are just as inspired as the originals, also known as "original autographs."

When God the Son, the Lord Jesus Christ, was on the earth, all He ever read from were copies. But He called them scripture. So we can be sure from Jesus Himself that trustworthy copies are scripture, too.

The King James Bible is an accurate translation of trustworthy copies of God's words. So we can trust that our King James Bible is God's preserved words in English.

LESSON 2

How Did God Inspire His Words?

STUDY VERSE –
2 PETER 1:21

"For the prophecy came not in old time by the will of man: but holy men of God spake as they were moved by the Holy Ghost."

God used at least 40 _____ men over 1500 years to write the scriptures. These were not *perfect men*, but they were *guided perfectly*. (The only perfect man was the Lord Jesus Christ.)

By Holy Men

These holy men spoke (and wrote) as they were _____ by the _____ _____.
But God did not move all these men in the same way. Let's see how some received God's words.

Moses was one of these holy men that God used to write the scripture.

13

READ EXODUS 4:29-31

"And Aaron spake all the words which the

LORD had _____ unto Moses…"

(verse 30).

Here we see that God _____ unto Moses.

Face to Face

Deuteronomy 34:10 tells of Moses:

"…whom the LORD knew _____

to _____."

With the Finger of God

READ DEUTERONOMY 9:9-11

The Lord delivered unto Moses two tables of stone written
with the "_____ of _____".

In a Dream or Vision

In Numbers 12:1-8, God said He will give His words to a
prophet (one who speaks for God) in a _____
and a _____ (verse 6).

A vision is a message from God that is seen by His
prophet. A dream from God is a vision His prophet sees
when asleep.

READ ISAIAH 1:1

"The _____ of Isaiah…"

READ DANIEL 2:19

"Then was the secret _____ unto

Daniel in a _____ _____."

By Revelation

READ EPHESIANS 3:3

"How that by _____ he

made known unto me the _____ ..."

Here God revealed a message, called "the mystery," to another man of God, the apostle Paul.

In Galatians 1:11-12, Paul said that his gospel (the words of God) came "by the _____ of Jesus Christ." Paul received the message of grace directly from the risen Lord Jesus Christ.

By the Holy Ghost

2 Peter 1:21 tells us that:

"... _____ men of God spake as they were

_____ by the _____ _____."

We have learned that God spoke or revealed the scriptures and holy men were moved by the Holy Ghost to write them. These scriptures were preserved perfectly in copies.

The "Very Words" or the "Basic Idea"?

The scriptures tell us that God inspired His very words and not just "the basic idea." **Every word** is given by inspiration of God!

READ EXODUS 20:1

"And God spake all these _____ ..."

READ PROVERBS 30:5-6

"Every _____ of God is _____ ..."

In verse 6, God gives a warning.

"_____ thou not unto his _____,

lest he _____ thee, and thou be

found a _____."

God's words are pure. We must not add to them!

READ PSALM 12:6-7

"The _____ of the LORD are pure

_____ : as silver tried in a furnace of

earth, _____ _____

times."

Purifying something seven times makes it *almost* perfect.
But God's words *are perfect*. Read Psalm 19:7

"The _____ (collection of rules) of the

LORD is _____ ..."

READ JEREMIAH 15:16

"Thy _____ were found, and I did

_____ them; and thy _____ was unto

me the joy and rejoicing of mine _____ ..."

Which are Most Important in the Bible?

(Circle one)

The Words / The Basic Ideas

In Matthew 4:4, Christ answered Satan with these words:

"…Man shall not live by bread alone, but by

_____ _____ that proceedeth

out of the mouth of God."

In John 6:63, Christ said:

"…the _____ that I speak unto you,

they are spirit, and they are life."

Christ does not say "the *thoughts* I convey to you," or "the *ideas.*" Christ very plainly says that His words are spirit and life.

In John 17:8, Christ spoke to His Father and said:

"For I have given unto them the _____

which thou gavest me;"

Many of the newer Bibles do not think that the **words** are important to God. So they try to convey what *they* think God meant, but *not what God actually said.* This is called "dynamic equivalence."

Which are important to God? (Circle the correct letter)

A. The very words, each and every word.

Or

B. The basic thoughts or ideas (dynamic equivalence)

The men who translated the manuscripts which came to be known as the 1611 KJV knew that **every word is important**. So they made sure to clearly translate each and every word. This is called "**formal equivalence**." We can rely on The King James Bible because the KJV was correctly translated, using "formal equivalence." Every word was carefully chosen.

Summary

God the Holy Ghost perfectly guided holy men to write down His words. He spoke to them face to face. He wrote them with His own finger (The Ten Commandments). Sometimes He gave a message to His prophets in dreams or visions. Other times He gave a revelation directly into His servant's mind.

God's written words are **pure**. There is nothing we can add to them to make them "more true." God's words are **perfect**. Nothing we can do to them will make them any better.

Some people make a big mistake. They make Bibles, but only write "the basic idea." This is called "dynamic equivalence." God does not want this. He wants us to carefully translate *every word*. This is called "formal equivalence."

The King James Bible is God's preserved words translated by "formal equivalence." So we can rely on our King James Bible as God's preserved words in English.

LESSON 3

God Preserved His Words

STUDY VERSES – PSALM 12:6-7
"The words of the LORD are pure words: as silver tried in a furnace of earth, purified seven times. Thou shalt keep them, O LORD, thou shalt preserve them from this generation for ever."

God's words are so important to Him that He tells us **He will preserve them**. God promised to keep the inspired text safe without error or loss.

God Promised to Preserve His Words For Ever

READ PSALM 12:6-7

"Thou shalt keep them, O LORD, thou shalt

_____ them from this

generation _____ _____" (verse 7).

READ PSALM 119:89

"_____ _____, O LORD, thy

_____ is settled in heaven."

READ 1 PETER 1:25

"But the _____ of the Lord

_____ _____ _____.

And this is the word which by the gospel is

preached unto you."

Without Error or Loss

READ MATTHEW 5:18

"…Till heaven and earth pass, one _____ or

one _____ shall in _____ wise pass

from the law, till _____ be fulfilled."

READ MATTHEW 24:35

"Heaven and earth shall pass away, but my

_____ shall not _____ _____."

(Note: God put these *exact same words* in Mark 13:31 and
Luke 21:33! That is how *important* these words are to
God.)

READ ISAIAH 30:8

"Now go, write it before them in a table, and

note it in a book, that it may be for the time to

come _____ _____ and _____."

God promised to preserve His words for ever. And He
promised that *not one single letter* would be lost! Is God
able to keep His promise?

(Circle the correct answer.)

Yes / No

God kept His promise to preserve His words.

How Important Are God's Words?

READ PSALM 138:2

"…for thou hast magnified thy _____

above all thy name."

Obviously, God's words are very important to Him.

READ JOB 23:12

"…I have esteemed the _____ of

his mouth more than my necessary food."

Job was right. God's words are more important than the food we need to live. Food keeps us alive for a *day*. But God's words help us live *forever*.

What have we learned so far?

God gave His words to mankind.	⟨ which means ⟩	God inspired His words.
God kept His words safe through all ages, without error or loss.	⟨ which means ⟩	God preserved His words.

But now we need to ask:

How did God Preserve His Words?

In Books

READ DEUTERONOMY 31:24

"And it came to pass, when Moses had made an end of writing the _____ of this law in a _____, until they were finished,"

READ VERSE 26

"Take this _____ of the law, and put it in the _____ of the _____ of the _____ of the LORD…"

The Lord had Moses write His words in a book and put it in a safe place, so His words would be read and copied faithfully by future generations.

READ AGAIN ISAIAH 30:8

"Now go, write it before them in a table, and note it _____ _____ _____, that it may be for the time to come for ever and ever."

READ JEREMIAH 30:2

"Thus speaketh the LORD God of Israel, saying, Write thee _____ the _____ that I have _____ unto thee _____ _____ _____."

READ REVELATION 1:11

"Saying, I am Alpha and Omega, the first and the last: and, What thou seest, write _____ ____ _____, and send it unto the seven churches which are in Asia…"

66 Books: One Bible

We have all **66** books that God gave by inspiration combined in **one** book, called the Bible. But remember: the 66 **original** books were *never* combined in one book! It was perfect copies of those books that were brought together.

The first **39** of those books are called the **Old Testament**. The last **27** are called the **New Testament**.

In Faithful Copies

READ DEUTERONOMY 17:18

"And it shall be, when he sitteth upon the throne of his kingdom, that he shall _____ him a _____ of _____ _____ in a _____ out of that which is before the priests the Levites:"

God preserved His words by having His people make **faithful copies** of them. Even the king of Israel had to make his own copy of Moses' writings!

In Accurate Translations

Once the Bible was finished, God's people carefully translated His words into many different languages. These translations were so accurate that the Bibles said the same thing in each language. They were God's words in their languages.

God's words were so precious to them that many people gave their lives rather than give up their Bibles.

Only What God Wants Us to Know

Old Testament

READ ROMANS 15:4

"For whatsoever things were written aforetime were written _____ _____

_____, that we through patience and comfort of the scriptures might have _____."

READ 1 CORINTHIANS 10:11

"Now all these things happened unto them for ensamples (examples): and they are written

_____ _____ _____

(warning), upon whom the ends of the world are come."

New Testament

READ JOHN 20:31

"But these are written, that ye might _____
that Jesus is the Christ, the Son of God; and that
_____ ye might have
_____ through his name."

READ JOHN 21:25

"And there are also many other things which
Jesus did, the which, if they should be written
every one, I suppose that even the world itself
could not contain the _____ that
should be _____. Amen."

Summary

God promised to preserve His words for ever and ever,
without one single error or one missing word or letter.
And God always keeps His promises.

God's words are very important to Him. He preserved His
words in 66 books that make up the Bible. The 39 books
of the Old Testament were written as examples and
warnings. Each book points us to hope in God.

The 27 books of the New Testament were written to
bring us to trust in Jesus Christ, who is God the Son and
Son of God.

The Lord made sure that godly believers made faithful

copies and accurate translations of the Bible. That way people all over the world could have God's words in their language.

Praise God that we have His preserved words in *our* language, the King James Bible!

LESSON 4

God Has a Purpose For His Words

STUDY VERSES –

2 TIMOTHY 3:16-17

"All scripture is given by inspiration of God, and is profitable for _____, for _____, for _____, for _____ in righteousness: That the man of God may be _____, _____ _____ unto all good works"

We know that God's words were given by inspiration. His faithful people wrote down what He told them to write. But **why** did God go to all that trouble? He answered that question in the verses above.

God's Words Are Profitable

For D_____

Doctrine means "teaching." When we want to know what God says about a particular subject, we turn to the Bible, not to man's opinions.

For R_____

Reproof is showing someone or something to be wrong. The Bible was written to tell us what **not** to do and what **not** to believe. That is *almost* as important as what we **must** believe!

For C_____

God's words tell us both what *is right* and how to *be right with God* again when we do things that are wrong. Do you want to understand right doctrine? Do you want to be in a healthy relationship with God? The Bible shows us both!

For I_____ in righteousness

The Bible teaches us how to maintain a right relationship with God. It also tells us what God calls "righteous." Many people ask, "What does God want me to do?" Pray and read your Bible. What God wants *never* goes against His Bible. Want a good place to start? Read the book of Romans.

That the Man of God May Be P_____

Everything God says is perfect. Everything God told us to do is perfect. Everything God planned for us is perfect. When God the Son came to earth as Jesus Christ, everything He did and said were perfect. **And all of this is in the Bible!** We cannot be perfect in this life. But if you want to know what "perfect" looks like and what a "perfect" person would do, read your Bible. God put it there for all to see.

Remember: if obeying the Bible completely could make a **person** perfect, then the **Bible** must be perfect, too. And God's preserved words are exactly that — *perfect*.

T_____ F_____ unto All Good Works

"Throughly" is the Classical English spelling of our word "thoroughly." This phrase means that everything we need to know so we can please God is in the Bible.

So God preserved His words to teach us what to believe and do, what *not* to believe and do, how to get right with God, how to *stay* right with God and what God calls "righteous." All of this helps us to be able to do what pleases God. So when we read God's words, pray to Him, trust Him and do what He says, we can *know* we are pleasing God.

God's Words Are Alive

READ HEBREWS 4:12

"For the word of God is _____, and

_____, and sharper than any

_____ _____ _____,

piercing even to the dividing asunder of soul and

spirit, and of the joints and marrow, and is a

_____ of the _____

and _____ of the heart."

"Quick" means "alive." The Bible is unlike any other book in the world. It is *alive*, because it is God's own words. And it's sharper than any two-edged _____. That means it not only shows others *their* sins; it also shows us *our* sins, too.

READ ISAIAH 55:11

"So shall my _____ be that goeth forth out

of my mouth: it shall not return unto me void,

but it shall _____ that

which I please, and it shall _____ in

the thing whereto I sent it."

God's words do *exactly* what He sent them to do. **God's words *never* fail.** So the more we trust and use God's own words, the more God will do His will in us.

God's Words Are Powerful to Save

READ ROMANS 1:16

"For I am not ashamed of the _____

of _____: for it is the _____

of _____ unto _____ to

every one that believeth; to the Jew first, and

also to the Greek."

What Is "the Word of God?"

Every word that God spoke is important. But when we talk about **all** of God's words as a group, we often call them "the word of God." The Bible is the *words* of God, but it is also referred to as the *"word of God."* The following are also called the "word of God."

The Gospel Is the Word of God

READ ROMANS 10:16-17

"But they have not all obeyed the _____.

For Esaias saith, Lord, who hath believed our

_____? So then faith cometh by

hearing, and hearing by the _____ of

_____."

NOW READ 2 TIMOTHY 2:8-9

"Remember that Jesus Christ of the seed of

David was raised from the dead according to my

_____: Wherein I suffer trouble, as an

evil doer, even unto bonds; but the _____

of _____ is not bound."

The Word of God is the Sword of the Spirit

READ EPHESIANS 6:17

"And take the helmet of salvation, and the

_____ of the Spirit, which is the

_____ of _____:"

God's preserved words are the Holy Spirit's sword! We have that sword, too. We have God's preserved words in English, the King James Bible. But we must be careful how we use that sword.

We Must Study the Word of God

READ 2 TIMOTHY 2:15

"_____ to shew thyself approved unto God, a _____ that needeth not to be ashamed, _____

_____ the word of truth."

READ 1 THESSALONIANS 2:13

"For this cause also thank we God without ceasing, because, when ye received the word of God which ye heard of us, ye received it _____ as the word of _____, but as it is in truth, the word of _____, which effectually _____ also in you that believe."

READ ROMANS 12:2

"And be not conformed to this world: but be ye _____ by the renewing of your _____, that ye may prove what is that _____, and _____, and _____, will of God."

As we study "the word of truth," we will better understand what God wants to do in our lives. As you have seen, the words of God are a two-edged sword. They cut *both ways*. They give us an answer to every one that asks us (1 Peter 3:15). But they also work like a surgeon in our own lives, making us more like the people God wants us to be.

Quick Quiz

We are commanded to rightly divide the word of truth. Could we study the word of truth if we didn't have it?

(Circle the correct answer.)

Yes / No

With all these great purposes that God has for His word, do you think it is possible that God lost it?

(Circle the correct answer.)

Yes / No

Summary

As 2 Timothy 3:16-17 says, God's words are profitable to teach, to show us both what is wrong and what is right, as well as how to *be* right with God again when we sin. They tell us how to be what God calls "righteous" and how to do good works for Him. His words are living and able to save us through the gospel. God's words are the sword the Holy Ghost uses to show others *their* sins and to show us *ours*. We must study the Bible and let it renew our minds so we may use God's words the way God wants us to.

Different Versions - Different Messages

2 Corinthians 2:17

KJV "For we are not as many, which **CORRUPT** the word of God:"

NIV "Unlike so many, we do not **PEDDLE** the word of God for profit."

These are <u>NOT</u> the same!

See page 36 for more on this verse.

LESSON 5

How Man Corrupted God's Words

STUDY VERSE – DEUTERONOMY 4:2:

"Ye shall not _____ unto the word which I command you, neither shall ye _____ ought from it, that ye may keep the commandments of the LORD your God which I command you."

We Must Not Add to or Take Away from God's Words!

READ PROVERBS 30:5-6

"_____ _____ of God is pure: he is a shield unto them that put their trust in him. _____ thou _____ unto _____ _____, lest he reprove thee, and thou be found a liar."

READ REVELATION 22:18-19

"For I testify unto every man that heareth the

_____ of the prophecy of this book, If

any man shall _____ unto these things, God

shall _____ unto him the _____

that are written in this book: And if any man

shall _____ _____ from the

_____ of the book of this prophecy, God

shall _____ _____ his part out of the

_____ of _____, and out of the holy

city, and from the things which are written in

this book."

If God warns us never to *add to* or *take away* from God's words, then what do you think the Devil does? He deceives men into thinking they can **make God's words better** by *adding to and taking away from* the words of the Holy Bible. *Don't be fooled!*

In Paul's day, Satan was already attacking the word of God. God wrote through Paul in 2 Corinthians 2:17:

"For we are not as _____, which

_____ the _____ of God:"

What is "corrupting the word of God?" Adding to and taking away from God's words!

As we begin comparing verses from the different versions, remember this: there are **no errors** in the 1611 Authorized

King James Version. It is God's perfectly preserved words and you can trust it completely. Watch very carefully what is *missing* from other versions, and what they add.

Is it Important to Answer This Question?

In Acts 8:26-40 God led Philip into the desert. There he met a powerful man from Ethiopia (the queen's eunuch) who was reading the book of Isaiah.

Philip asked the Ethiopian a question: "Understandest what thou readest?" (Acts 8:30).

The eunuch answered, "How can I, except some man should guide me?" Then he invited Philip to answer his Bible questions. From that verse Philip preached Jesus to the Eunuch (Acts 8:31-35).

Soon they came to some water, probably a desert oasis. Then the Ethiopian eunuch asked Philip a vital question: "See, here is water; what doth hinder me to be baptized?" (Acts 8:36)

This is an important question. What must happen before he could be baptized as a Christian? People ask this all the time.

Let's see how the New International Version answers it:

> "38And he gave orders to stop the chariot. Then both Philip and the eunuch went down into the water and Philip baptized him." (NIV)

Philip answered the Ethiopian's *other* questions. Why didn't he answer *this* question? Wait a minute! That's verse 38. Where is verse 37?

It's in your King James Bible! Acts 8:37 says:

> "And Philip said, _____ thou _____
> with all thine heart, thou mayest. And he
> answered and said, I _____ that
> Jesus Christ is the Son of God."

So Philip *did* answer that question, but it's *missing* from the NIV.[1] Is that important? *You bet it is!* It's the **only verse in the entire Bible** that answers this important question.

Why Did Jesus Rebuke Them?

In Luke 9:51-56 Jesus needed to go to Jerusalem. The quickest way there was through a village in Samaria. But the Samaritans refused to let Him go through their village. James and John were furious! They asked Jesus,

> "Lord, wilt thou that we command fire to come
> down from heaven, and consume them, even as
> Elias (Elijah) did?" (Luke 9:54).

What did Jesus answer? Let's check the New Revised Standard Version:

> "55But he turned and rebuked them. 56Then
> they went on to another village." (NRSV)

---

[1]Acts 8:37 is also missing from the New Living Translation (NLT), New Revised Standard (NRSV) and Revised Standard (RSV). Other versions put brackets around it or put it in italics, to act as if it isn't really scripture.

Don't you wish we could have been there that day, to know why Jesus rebuked James and John? This was a perfect opportunity to teach His disciples. Why didn't He?

But He did!

READ LUKE 9:55-56 IN YOUR **KJV!**

"But he turned, and rebuked them, and said, Ye know not what manner of _____ ye are of. For the Son of man is _____ come to _____ men's lives, but to _____ them. And they went to another village."

The Lord Jesus used this as an opportunity to teach **why** He came to this earth. His *first* coming was to *save*. His *second* coming will be to *judge*. God's important words are *missing* from corrupted versions!

Where Did All These Bibles Come From?

Modern Bible versions that are **missing** God's words go all the way back to manuscripts written in Alexandria, Egypt. Only about 44 of them have been found. Most are little scraps of paper or a few pages long. Three of them look like huge Bibles. They contain the New Testament, the Old Testament, and even have apocryphal books mixed in. (They are called **Sinaiticus**, **Vaticanus** and **Alexandrinus**.) The men who wrote them thought they could make God's words "better." So they **added** some *words, phrases*, and even whole *books*. And they also **took away** other *words*, whole *verses* and even some entire *chapters!*

But that is not all. They could **not agree** with each other on what should be put **into** their Bibles. So Alexandrian manuscripts don't even agree with **each other!**

When the Roman Emperor Constantine (312-337 AD) pretended to be a Christian, he sent to Alexandria for 50 perverted Greek Bibles. A monk named Jerome later translated those fake Greek Bibles into Latin by 405 AD. That is called the **Roman Catholic Latin Vulgate**.

In the 1800s, when modern "scholars" claimed they could "fix" the Bible, what do you suppose they used? Those perverted Greek manuscripts from Alexandria, the same kind that the Roman Catholics used to make **their** perverted Bible!

But God always keeps His promises. He preserved His words in a city called Antioch of Syria, where the disciples were first called Christians (Acts 11:26). There, they translated the complete Bible into Old Latin and Syriac by about 150 AD! And from Antioch they went all over the known world. Bible believers made more exact copies and faithful translations of both the Old Testament and the New Testament.

When godly men got together in England from 1604 to 1611 to make an accurate English Bible, what do you suppose they used? Those preserved Bibles, of course! They very carefully compared these translations and copies, and even some earlier English Bibles. And God helped them write a perfect English translation of the Bible. It is known as the "Authorized Version," the "1611 King James Bible," the "Holy Bible" or simply the "KJV." So the King James Bible you hold in your hands is God's preserved words in English.

Turning God's Words Upside-Down!

READ PHILIPPIANS 2:5-6

"Let this mind be in you, which was also in

Christ Jesus: Who, being in the form of God,

thought it _____ _____

to be _____ with God:"

If you or I wanted to be equal with God, that would be robbery. We have no business pretending to be God. We're not God! That would be stealing, or robbing what belongs only to God. But Jesus knew being God was not robbery at all for Him. *Jesus was God!*

But verse 6 in the New American Standard Version says the *opposite*!

"who, although He existed in the form of God, did not regard equality with God **a thing to be grasped.**" (NASV)

This is a lie! **Jesus never stopped being God!** He was Emmanuel — "God with us." He entered a body and walked on the earth — but He was still God! **Of course** He grasped — or held onto — His equality to God. He never stopped *being God!*

Is Jesus God's Son — or Only His "Servant"?

READ ACTS 3:25-26

"Ye are the children of the prophets, and of the covenant which God made with our fathers, saying unto Abraham, And in thy _____ shall all the kindreds of the earth be blessed. Unto you first God, having raised up his

_____ _____, sent him to bless you, in turning away every one of you from his iniquities."

God told Abraham that *his son* (his "seed") would bless the people of the earth. In the same way, God raised up *His Son Jesus* to bless the world by turning them away from their sins! This was a powerful message: Jesus, God's Son, was sent to earth to bless us. Notice that they didn't hide the truth, but said it clearly: **Jesus is God's Son!**

But wait! Read verse 26 in the New King James Version!

"To you first, God, having raised up His **Servant** Jesus, sent Him to bless you, in turning away every one of you from your iniquities." (NKJV)

"Son" and "Servant" are not the same! The New King James version demotes Jesus from being the *exalted* Son of God to a *lowly* servant, like any sinful human.

Other modern perversions do even more. They actually ***remove*** the name of ***Jesus*** from the verse!

Do You Want to Be a Person of Great Faith?

READ HEBREWS 11:6

"But without _____ it is impossible to

_____ him: for he that cometh

to God must _____ that

he is, and that he is a rewarder of them that

_____ _____ him."

Have you ever seen or read about a man or woman of great faith? Their lives are an amazing testimony to God. How about you? Have you ever wanted to be like them? The only way is by exercising your *faith* in God. How do we do that?

READ ROMANS 10:17

"So then _____ cometh by

_____, and _____ by

the _____ of _____."

If you read God's words and *believe them*, He will increase your faith. That's a promise from God Himself. And unlike modern Bible versions, *God cannot lie.*

Summary

God warns us not to *add to* or *take away from* His holy words. But the Devil does, all the time! Satan does everything he can to corrupt the word of God, especially through modern Bible versions. But "modern Bibles" are not truly modern. They really come from ancient corrupted manuscripts out of Alexandria, Egypt. And they were later used to make the perverted Roman Catholic Bible.

But God kept His promises. Starting with Bible believers in Antioch of Syria, He preserved His words through exact copies and faithful translations. Your King James Bible is exactly that. It is God's perfectly preserved words, translated into English. We can put our faith in them. And as we read and believe them, we will become people of great faith.

FOR MORE INFORMATION

For further study on the Bible version issue, you may want to purchase the following books. Most Christians know there are many versions but are not aware of the problems with the new versions.

Available from Chick Publications (www.chick.com):

Answers to Your Bible Version Questions
by David W. Daniels. ISBN 0-7589-0507-6

Did the Catholic Church Give Us the Bible?
by David W. Daniels. ISBN 0-7589-0579-3

Final Authority
by William P. Grady. ISBN 0-9628809-1-4

The Language of the King James Bible
by Gail Riplinger. ISBN 0-9635845-1-0

Let's Weigh the Evidence
by Barry Burton. ISBN 0-937958-17-4

New Age Bible Versions
by G. A. Riplinger. ISBN 0-9635845-0-2

Other helpful books:

A Testimony Founded for Ever
by James H. Sightler, MD. ISBN 0-9673343-0-6

The King James Version Defended
by Edward F. Hills ISBN 0-915923-00-9

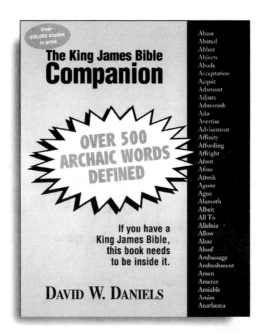
Understand what you are reading?

What do you do when you are reading your Bible, and you come across an unfamiliar word? Get out a big dictionary and look it up? Or just read on, hoping to get something more familiar in the next verse? Most people read on, and don't fully understand what they have just read.

Put this little 24-page book into the back of your Bible. When you see a word that isn't familar, just look it up. These simple definitions of over 500 uncommon words found in the Bible will help you truly *__understand__* what you are reading!

David Daniels, B.A., M.Div., is trained in Bible and linguistics. After twenty years of intense study, he has concluded that the King James Bible is God's preserved words in English.

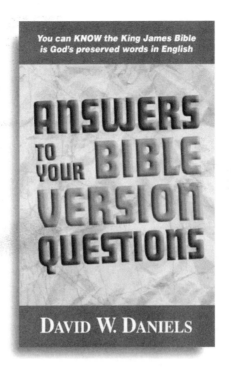

You can KNOW the King James Bible is God's preserved words in English

ANSWERS TO YOUR BIBLE VERSION QUESTIONS

DAVID W. DANIELS

Did God preserve His words?
Or does my Bible contain errors?

Here, respected linguist David Daniels provides easy-to-understand answers to a wide variety of difficult questions so-called "experts" throw at the King James version. The result? Proof that the King James Bible is God's preserved words in English.

If you want to defend the KJV, or learn which Bible you can trust, the answers are here. *221 pages, paperback*

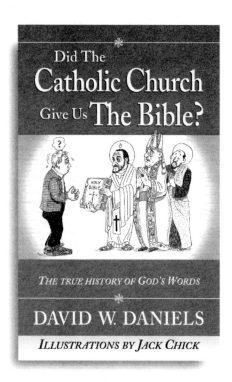

Did The **Catholic Church** Give Us **The Bible?**

THE TRUE HISTORY OF GOD'S WORDS

DAVID W. DANIELS

ILLUSTRATIONS BY JACK CHICK

Written a down-to-earth style, with cartoon illustrations by Jack Chick, this book shows the two different histories of the Bible. One is of God preserving His words through His people. The other is of the devil using the Roman Catholic church to pervert God's words through her "scholars."

Do YOU have God's preserved words, or a corrupted counterfeit?

Learn how we got modern Bibles and why the Bibles Rome gave us are counterfeits, designed to eliminate God's preserved words in English, the KJV. *160 pages, paperback*

Available from:

CHICK PUBLICATIONS
PO Box 3500, Ontario, Calif. 91761
Order online at: **www.chick.com**